编　　写：楼望皓
总体设计：丁晓仑
责任编辑：刘　振
英文翻译：刘岭泉
摄　　影：楼望皓　阿斯力汗·巴根　刘　振　宋士敬　赵君安　沈　桥
　　　　　图尔迪　涂苏别克　阿不力孜·阿布都拉　焦力·卡德尔
　　　　　李　扬　王德钧　丁晓仑　丁晓昆　向　京　张军戈　于　雷
　　　　　加尔肯　陈晓辉　韩连赟　亚力坤　晏　先　沈天翔　侯　建
　　　　　约提克尔·尼加提　张守礼　毕亚丁　范书财　丽　玛
　　　　　艾拉提·买买提依明　李芝庭　杨新才

Writer: Lou WangHao

Designer: Ding XiaoLun

Chief editor: Liu　Zhen

English by: Liu　LinQian

Photographer: Lou WangHao　A Si Li Han · Ba Gen　Liu Zhen　Song ShiJing　Zhao JunAn
　　　　　　　Shen Qiao　Tu ErDi　Tu Su Bie Ke　A Bu Li Zi · A Bu Du La　Li Yang
　　　　　　　Jiao Li · Ka De Er　Shen TianXiang　Wang DeJun　Ding XiaoLun　Ding XiaoKun
　　　　　　　Jia ErKen　Chen XiaoHui　Han LianYu　Ya LiKun　Xiang Jing　Yan Xian
　　　　　　　Yue Ti Ke Er · Ni Jia Ti　Yu Lei　Zhang ShouLi　Hou Jian　Bi YaDing
　　　　　　　Li Ma　Ai La Ti · Mai Mai Ti Yi Ming　Li ZhiTing　Yang XingCai　Zhang junge

中国·新疆
民俗大观

The Grand Sight of China
Xin Jiang's Folk-customs

新疆美术摄影出版社

婚　嫁　　　　民居交通　　　　饮　食　　　　服　饰

MARRIAGE　　　The living and traffic　　　Food and drink　　　Clothing and dressing

工艺品　　体　育　　丧　葬　　人生礼仪　　节　日

Craftwork　　SPORT　　FUNERAL　　ETIQUETTE　　FESTIVAL

70　　82　　94　　106　　118

婚 嫁
MARRIAGE

婚嫁是人生中的一件大事，也是爱情的结晶。新疆少数民族的婚俗是十分隆重热烈的。从说亲、订亲到婚礼都要举行专门的仪式，而每种仪式都表达了老一辈对青年一代的祝福和期望，同时，也表达了男女之间的忠贞的爱情。

在少数民族的婚俗中，虽然还保持着宗教的色彩，但这种色彩已逐渐淡去，青年男女已自由恋爱和结合，并得到长辈们的支持。

婚礼的场面虽然热烈，但也是一件严肃的事情，婚姻本身就是繁衍后代的一种合法的手续，那么,各民族怎么会不慎重地对待这件终身大事呢?

Marriage is a great event of life, and also the result of love. The wedding ceremonies of Xin Jiang's minority are very grand and lively. In the period From matchmaking, engagement to the wedding ceremony, some special ceremonies have to be hold. Each ceremony is the good wishes of the old generations to the young people, and expresses the loyal love of the marring couple.

In the wedding custom of minorities, some religious habits remained, but are fading out gradually. The young people love each other by their own choice, and get married supported by their elder generations

Though the wedding ceremony is very warm and busy, it is a serious thing anyway, all nationalities treat this event with great discretion

维吾尔族小伙子穿上了传统的新婚礼服。
This Uigur chap wearing the traditional wedding dress

要和养育自己的父母分开了, 新娘在"尼卡"仪
式上哭了起来。
The Uigur bride is crying on the Nika's ceremony,
for that she has to part with her parents.

新郎给新娘带上结婚戒指。
The bridegroom is putting on the
ring on the finger of the bride.

迎亲时, 妈妈要给女儿戴上盖头。
Mother should putting on the hood for her
daughter when sending out the procession to
receive the people from bridegroom's family.

新郎和新娘步入婚礼。
The bride and bridegroom are coming
into the place of wedding ceremony.

在"尼卡"仪式上，新郎和新娘要抢着吃蘸满盐水的馕，表
达对爱情的忠诚。
On "Nika" wedding ceremony, the bridegroom and bridge have
to grab and eat the Nang which has been dipped in the saltwater,
to express their faithfulness to the love.

新郎和新娘要在伴郎和伴娘陪同下才在婚礼上出现。
The bride and bridegroom will show themselves up only
under the company of groomsman and bridesmaid.

在结婚之前，男方的母亲要请来女宾做客，
商量订亲的事宜，并确定结婚日期。

Before her son getting marry, the mother would invite the female guests
to discuss the matters of engagement, and confirm the date of marrying.

向儿媳妇赠送礼品
Presenting the gifts to the daughter-in-law.

美丽的维吾尔族新娘。The beautiful Uigur bride.

在正式婚礼的当天或前一天，都要举行〝尼卡〞的宗教仪式。
A Nika's religious ceremony will be hold in the same day of the
wedding ceremony or a day before.

家人高兴地迎接来宾。
The family members receive the guests gladly.

按着传统习惯，用地毯把新娘抬起来。
The bride is lifted up in a carpet by the traditional custom.

又一位姑娘要出嫁了，乡亲们纷纷前来祝贺。
Another girl is going to get married, the villagers are coming to celebrate.

哈萨克人用马驮着花毡、箱子、被子等彩礼。
These Kazaks are carrying the betrothal gifts of
flower felts, boxes and quilts with horses.

临出嫁之前，老人总要向自己的女儿叮嘱几句，希
望她孝敬公婆，夫妻相爱。
Before getting married, the old parents would urge their
daughter to be respectful and filial to her father-in-law
and mother-in-law, and love her husband.

哈萨克人在女儿出嫁时，要带上陪嫁的彩礼到新郎家。这是刚刚下马的新娘走向新房。
When their daughters are getting married, the Kazaks will bring the betrothal gifts to the bridegroom's family. This is the bride just dismounting the horse going towards the bridal chamber.

新娘进入毡房后，不能揭开面纱，要经过一定的仪式后，才能揭开。
The bride's veil can not be immediately uncovered when the bride has come into the felt chamber until some ceremonies have been hold.

要把彩礼向大伙儿展示。
The betrothal gifts have to be shown to the people.

哈萨克人女儿出嫁，还要陪嫁马匹。
The horses are needed as the betrothal gifts when the daughters of Kazak people are getting married.

15

聆听阿訇的教诲　Listening to the imam's tuition.

塔吉克族新娘要踩着白布进入新房，以表示少女的纯洁。
When a Tajikkazak bride is entering the bridal chamber, she should step on the white cloth to show that the she is virgin.

维吾尔族乡亲十分热情地把钱、布料和馕送到有喜事的人家里。
The Uigur villagers are very warm to send the money, cloth and home-made Nang to the home of happy event.

柯尔克孜族妇女在布置新房。
Khalkhas women are decorating the bridal chamber.

柯尔克孜族的新郎和新娘全家人为他们结成伴侣祝福。
The Khalkhas families of bride and bridegroom blessing good luck for the new couple.

维吾尔族的婚礼上，大家跳舞祝贺。
The people are dancing and celebrating in the wedding ceremony of Uigur nationality.

俄罗斯人的婚礼隆重而热烈，人们频频举杯，向新郎新娘祝贺。
The wedding ceremony of Russia is grand and heat, people are toasting to the bride and bridegroom.

锡伯族新郎新娘结婚后要敬火神。
The bride and bridegroom of Xibo nationality should worship the God of Fire after getting married.

锡伯族新郎新娘要向父母谢恩。
The bride and bridegroom of Xibo nationality should express their thanks to their parents.

达斡尔族新郎新娘要拜老人。
The bride and bridegroom of Dawoer nationality should make a courtesy call to their old generations.

塔吉克族的婚礼上，人们翩翩起舞。
People of Tajik are dancing in the wedding ceremony.

让新郎和新娘喝上一碗酸奶，表示祝福。
Give the bride and bridegroom a drink of a cup of sour milk, to express the good wishes.

哈萨克族也有拦亲的习俗，迎亲人必须留下礼品，才能放行。
The Kazak nationality has the custom to stop the bridegroom's procession receiving the bride, and the gifts are asked before allowing to go.

柯尔克孜族的婚俗中也有拦亲的习俗。
Khalkhas nationality has the same marrying custom of stopping the bridegroom's procession receiving the bride.

塔吉克族新郎一家人准备迎娶新娘。
The Tajik bridegroom's family are preparing
to receive the bride.

塔吉克族新郎和新娘的脸上还要点上吉祥
的白点，表达了他们相爱到底的决心。

The faces of bride and bridegroom of Tajik nationality should be dotted
with white spots of lucky, to express their will of a long-lasting love.

出嫁前，用头巾盖在头上，家人和姐妹们为之祝福。
Before getting married, the bride's head is covered with hood, the family and sisters blessing good luck for her.

骆驼驮来了嫁妆。
The camels are carrying the dower to here.

喝上一碗牛奶，祝愿新郎新娘的爱情像牛奶那样纯洁。
Drink a cup of milk, wishing the love of the new couple as pure as the milk.

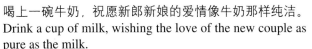

在信仰伊斯兰教的民族中，婚礼宴席上往往是男女分席。

In the nationalities believing in Islam, men and women are separated on the wedding dinners.

各民族的喜事都有一个共同的特点，那就是两个人的婚事，牵动着大家的心。人们在祝愿新人幸福时，自己也获得了幸福。

The marital events of all nationalities have the same character, i.e. the marriage of two people attracts the hearts of all people. When people are blessing the happy of others, they get the happy themselves.

民居交通
The living and traffic

特殊的地理环境和历史，使新疆的居住条件和交通状况，与内地大不相同，这些独具民族特色的住宅和交通工具，使人们享受到一种别样的乐趣。

新疆是典型的大陆性气候，冬季漫长。针对这种情况，维吾尔人设计了窗小墙厚的砖木结构的房屋。在逐草放牧的牧区，各种毡房成了牧民的乐园。不管结构如何，但建造上都讲究各民族不同的特色和风格。

交通落后的新疆，诞生了以牛、马、骆驼、毛驴为动力的代步和运输工具，虽然速度慢了些，但十分安全和廉价。在偏远的地区，人们仍然可以看到这种古朴的踪影。

The living and traffic condition in Xin Jiang are greatly different from the inland as its special geographic condition and history background. These distinctive houses and vehicles give people a special enjoyment

Xin Jiang is in a typical continental weather, the winter is long. In this case, Xin Jiang people have built the houses of brick-and-timber construction with small windows and thick walls. In the pasturing areas, various kinds of felt houses have become the paradise. No matter how the structure is, the feature and style of the construction are varied between different nationalities.

The traffic in Xin Jiang is undeveloped, the ox, horse, camel and donkey are their main vehicles of walk and transportation without pollution. Their speed is slow, but safe and cheap. In the remote areas, these ancient scenes are seen often.

维吾尔族的住所讲究有长廊,并在屋檐和廊柱上雕有花纹或绘有图案，显得富丽堂皇。

The living of Uigur emphasizes on a long corridor, and carve or paint the patterns on the eaves or columns, making the decoration magnificent.

墙壁用的砖上，也雕刻有花纹。

The bricks on the wall are also carved with patterns.

维吾尔族的庭院一般都栽花种树，不仅调节空气，还美化了环境。

Most of the courtyards of Uigur houses are planted with trees and flowers, this is good for both atmosphere and environment.

住所修建离地面较高，可以防潮，所以大都设有台阶。墙壁多用硫璃砖贴面。
The Uigur houses are built higher above the ground, damp-proofed, so most of them have the steps. The walls are covered with color glazed tiles.

维吾尔族不仅注重室外的装璜，同时也十分注重室内的装饰，在客厅内的迎面墙壁上设有壁龛，壁龛里都摆放富有民族特色的工艺品，一进屋里就会感到一种浓郁的民族艺术的气息。
The Uigurs not only emphasize on outdoor decorations, but also indoor upholstering. There are tabernacles in the head-on side of the wall, each tabernacle has the craftworks of the nationality, a strong breath of folk art is meeting the face.

用卵石砌成的平房。
The bungalows built up by screes.

维吾尔族民宅中，窗户的装饰也十分重要，整个建筑风格都很配套。
The windows of Uigur houses are also well-decorated, the whole construction styles are matching well with each other.

和田地区的民宅与其它地区不一样。在大屋中设有天井，中间的大厅既是客厅又是卧室，两侧的房间有厨房和库房，也有卧室。这种设计，冬暖夏凉，且防风防沙。

The civil houses in Hetian area are different from the other areas. There is a skylight in a big room, the lobby in the center is both a meeting room and bedroom, and there are kitchen room and storeroom as well as bedroom on both sides. This design is warm in winter and cool in summer, and sand-blowing proofed.

这是伊犁地区典型的维吾尔族院落，葡萄架上房，葡萄架后还有花卉和果树。主人不时给花卉浇水、剪枝，显得十分安逸。

This is a typical Uigur courtyard in Yili area. The grape trees are covering over the racks, and there are flowers and fruit trees behind the racks. The owner is watering the plants here and there, and pruning some trees, how an easy living.

维吾尔族人喜欢在廊檐前搭葡萄架，夏天既可遮风雨，又可乘凉歇息。廊檐下摆上桌子，铺上地毯，可作宽敞的餐厅。

Uigurs like to put up a grape rack over the corridor, it can shelter the wind and rain in summer, and enjoy the cool and rest. Put a table and cover a carpet on the corridor, it can treat the guests or serve as a spacious dinning-room.

俄罗斯人的住房。The houses of Russian.

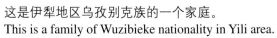

锡伯族的老房。
The old houses of Xibo nationality.

这是伊犁地区乌孜别克族的一个家庭。
This is a family of Wuzibieke nationality in Yili area.

毡房被称为〝草原上的白宫〞。这种易搬迁的毡房，不仅外观独特，而且内部摆设合理，适于牧区生活。

The felt houses of the minorities are call"The white houses on grassland". These houses are quake-proofed and easy to be moved, their appearance is unique, their interior is properly furnished, suitable for the live in pasturing area.

哈萨克等民族的毡房拆迁容易，两个小时就可以安装起来。
The felt houses of Kazak are easy to be removed, and be re-built
within two hours.

毡房和平房都布置的艺术化。虽然外面荒凉，但家里却是色彩缤纷。
The felt houses and bungalows are all artistically decorated, though their
exterior looks some desolated, but their interior is lively and colorful.

毡房内的被、毡、床、枕头等都表现出牧民的艺术天赋。

The quilts, felts, beds, pillows in the felt houses show up the artistic genius of herdsmen.

建造一座毡房是非常费事的。要打羊毛(右上)、擀毡子(下)、编制彩带(左上)、绣花(右下)等多种工艺，另外还得做支架。

To build up a felt house takes a lots of things to do. Need beating wool(bottom left), rolling felts(top left), weaving color tapes(bottom right), and embroidering the patterns on the felts(left), etc. And also need to erect a support.

在天山北麓，牧民还根据当地木材多的特点，建造了各种各样的木屋。

On the northern mountain foot of Tian Shan, the herdsmen have built many various wooden houses as the forest area there is.

塔吉克人的房内有五根柱子，屋中有天窗，天窗要有五层木板撑起来。有天窗的房子是客厅和卧室。

There are five posts in a Tajik house, and a skylight in a room, the skylight is supported by 5 layers of boards. The room has a skylight is the meeting room and bedroom .

马 车 Carriages

毛驴车 Donkey carts

在牧区没有公路的情况下，骆驼仍是牧民的运载工具。这是牧民在转场。
When no roads are built in the pasturing area, the camels are still a mean of delivery. The herdsmen are shifting the pasture.

别看这个小家伙，他可以驾驭比他大几倍的骆驼。
See this small guy, he can rein the camel several folds bigger than him.

在阿勒泰地区，一到冬天，这种雪橇是他们出门首选的代步工具。
In the Aletai area, when winter is coming, this kind of sledge is their preferred walk tool.

牛 车 Oxcarts

独木舟 Canoes

饮　食
Food and drink

　　新疆少数民族占总人口的62%以上。长期以来，由于受到宗教、文化、历史、地理环境等诸多因素的影响，因而各民族饮食心理、饮食礼仪以及在饮食文化上都有不同的差异。

　　信仰伊斯兰教的少数民族禁食猪肉。以牛羊肉和乳制品为主的新疆传统风味小吃，是各民族饮食文化的主题。花色品种和风味也在全国独树一帜。

　　除此以外，以当地产品加工的各种创新菜，也基本形成体系，各民族之间的文化交流，也促使了新疆少数民族饮食文化结构的变化，使餐桌上的食品更加丰富多彩。

　　旅游在新疆，吃也在新疆，不妨您来试试。

　　The number of the minorities in Xin Jiang is above 62% to the total population. From the history, influenced by the religion, culture, historical events, geographical elements, the habits, etiquettes and culture of the food and drink are different between all minorities.

　　The port is fasting for the Islam believers. The Xin Jiang's flavor foods mainly made by beef, mutton and milk are the main subject of all nationalities' food & drink culture. Their varieties and the tastes are distinctive in the country.

　　Except this, the new foods made by local products have formed their own varieties. The culture exchanges between all nationalities have changed at some degree the Xin Jaing minorities' food & drink culture, making the dishes on the table more rich and colorful.

　　Touring in Xin Jiang and eating in Xin Jiang, please come and have a try.

抓饭是维吾尔、哈萨克、乌孜别克等民族的拿手好饭。其原料有大米、洋葱、羊肉、清油、胡萝卜等。营养丰富，可称"十全大补"饭。由于原料不同，可做成十几种抓饭。

"Grasping food" is a popular food of Uigur and Wuzibieke nationalities. Its materials include rice, onion, mutton, oil and carrot, full of all kinds nutrition. With different materials, a dozen of "grasping foods" can by made.

薄皮包子 Thin-skinned stuffed buns

果西格尔德（肉馅窝窝馕）
Guoxigeerde (meat stuffed Nang)

帕尔木达（烤包子） Paermuda (Baked stuffed bun)

维吾尔族的各种包子也是美味的食品，其原料主要以肉和洋葱为馅。上图为厨师在包包子。
Various kinds of stuffed buns are all delicious food of Uigur, they are mainly stuffed by meat and onion. The chef is making the stuffed buns.

风靡全国的烤羊肉串，受到广大群众的青睐。
The grilled mutton cluster" is well-known to the all country, people like it very much.

"烤全羊"是新疆的一道名菜。味鲜可口，令人垂涎欲滴。
"Full-broiled sheep"is a famous food in Xin Jiang. It's so delicious .

"烤全驼"是古老的传统佳肴，把整峰骆驼放在特制的土炉子里烤，再加上各种佐料，使味道独特而鲜美。

The "broiled full camel" is a traditional food. Put the whole camel on a special earth stove, and add some spices, the taste would be unique and fresh.

住在塔里木河畔的维吾尔人常常以河里的大鲤鱼作为美肴，烤而食之。
The Uigurs living along the riversides of Talimu river usually catch the carps and broil them, to be their delicious food.

馕包肉是用馕和肉组成的佳肴。把煮熟的肉夹在馕中，再配上肉汤，其味更加可口。
"Nang meat" is a good food made by Nang and meat. Put the cooked meat in the middle of Nang, and add some broth, it tastes delicious.

馕是新疆少数民族的主食，天山南北都有馕房。
The Nang is the main food of Xin Jiang minorities, there are Nang shops all over the north and south of Tianshan areas.

馕的巴扎(集市)和众多的馕品种。
Baja(market) of Nang(bun) and the
various kinds of Nang.

拉条子(拌面)是深受中外游客欢迎的快餐。
"Pulling strip" is a good snack favored by the tourists of Chinese and foreigners.

哈萨克族妇女用小火慢慢煮肉，使肉又嫩又鲜。
The Kazak women are cooking the meat with slow fire, to make the meat tender and fresh.

哈萨克人吃肉讲究礼仪，要把羊头和大腿等部位的肉先敬长者，表示尊重。
There are some formalities when Kazaks eating meat. The parts of sheep's head and thighs have to be presented to the superiors firstly to express their respect.

少数民族糕点荟萃。The collection of various minority cakes.

扁馓子 The flat Sanzi

点心 Refreshments

包尔萨克 Baoersake

圆包尔萨克 Round baoersake

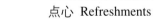

少数民族的糕点食品十分丰富。请品尝馓子。
How abundant the minority's cakes and food are. Please have a taste of these Sanzi.

厨师根据新疆的土特产，创新了许多菜肴，丰富了新疆菜系。
The chefs have made many good dishes out of Xin Jiang's special local products.

哈萨克族妇女在炸包尔萨克。
The kazak women are frying the baoersake.

俄罗斯族的面包真够香的。
How spicy the Russian bread is.

自制的部分糕点和糖果。
Some of cakes and candies self-made.

俄罗斯族的蛋糕。The Russian cakes.

哈萨克、柯尔克孜等民族在宰羊吃肉时，要举行一种"巴塔"的仪式。客人要祈祷，祝主人人畜两旺，好运不断。

The ceremony of "Bata" should be hold when Kazak and Khalkhas are slaughtering and eating the mutton. The guests should pray good luck for the hosts.

俄罗斯族的"苏波汤"，其味鲜美。 The Russia nationality's "Subo soup" is very delicious.

新疆乳资源十分丰富，少数民族喜欢食用牛、马、羊、骆驼的乳汁，并用乳汁做成各种乳制品。

Xinjian has rich milk resource, the minorities like to drink the milks from cow, horse, sheep and camel, and also make milk products with these milks.

人们把牛奶或羊奶放在皮桶或木桶里,让其发酵,做成酸奶或奶疙瘩。
The people put the cow's milk or sheep's milk into the leather or wood pails, to make it ferment, then the sour milk or milk lump is produced.

奶茶是牧民一日三餐离不开的饮料。
The milk tea is the necessity of every meal.

蒙古族牧民用牛奶或羊奶可做成醇香的奶酒,用来自饮或待客。
The Mongolian herdsmen can make out the mellow milk wine from cow milk or sheep milk, to treat the guests or drink by themselves.

马奶是营养丰富的饮料,既可防暑,又可抗病,深受牧民欢迎。
The horse milk is a nutritious drink, either can prevent sunstroke or resist the illness, it is the favorite of herdsmen.

丰富的食品，必须有丰富的餐具。每件用具制
作都很精美，既是餐具，又是一件工艺品。
The abundant food needs good tableware. Every
tableware is lovely and exquisite, either a tool or
a craftwork .

除了鲜食水果外，还晾制成干果。
Except eating fresh fruit, the dry fruit are also been made.

到了隆冬，新疆人冒着严寒，品尝哈密瓜，其情趣别有一番。
When in winter, the Xin Jiang people tasting Hami melon in the cold, what a distinctive feeling.

服　饰
Clothing and dressing

　　新疆少数民族男子骠悍，女子婀娜多姿，妩媚动人，她们除了天生的丽质外，多彩的服装配饰的衬托也是一个重要的原因。

　　严寒的冬季，使男人们选择了众多的皮衣、皮帽、皮靴，这种独特的设计，不仅烘托了男人们骁勇的体格，而且也增添了不少雄风。

　　艾德莱斯绸的衣裙，变化多样的头饰，使新疆少数民族的女子更加楚楚动人，令人心醉。

　　花卉、图案浸透在男人女人的各式服饰之中，而各种各样的服装设计，也完全适应了新疆的环境和气候。虽然新疆有大面积单色的沙漠和戈壁，但这些流动的服饰，却给新疆增添了悦目的色彩。

　　The men of Xin Jian minorities are strong and brave, while the women are lovely and attractive. Except they born beautifully, the colorful dress is a good setting off of their beautiful shapes

　　In the severe winter, the men select more leather coats, leather caps, and leather boots. This particular design has displayed fully the men's strong and brave

　　The dress made of Aiderliesi silk, and the various headgear, making the Xin Jiang minority girls more lovely and attractive

　　Flowers and various patterns are embroidered on the clothes of men and women. All kinds of clothes designs are matching the Xin Jiang's special environment and weather. Though the great extent of desert or gobi is single color, these moving clothes adding more flowery colors on it.

绚丽多彩的各民族服饰。
The floweriness of minority clothing.

花帽、皮帽、裙子、长辫都是维吾尔族青年妇女喜爱的装饰。
Flower hat, leather hat, skirt and long plait are the means of beauty of young Uigur women.

艾德莱斯绸是维吾尔族妇女首选的绸料。用这种绸做成裙子，使维吾尔族妇女更显得楚楚动人。

The Aideliesi silk is the preferred of Uigur women. It makes the women more lovely and attractive to wear the skirts making out of this kind of silk.

年纪稍大的维吾尔族妇女虽然也穿裙子，但单色的头巾却是不可少的。
The older Uigur women wear the skirts too, but the single color hood is necessary.

于田维吾尔族妇女的箭服。
The "arrow dress" of Uigur women in Yutian.

于田的小帽可能是世界上最小的帽子。
The Yutian small hat should be the smallest hat in the world.

传统的柯尔克孜族青年妇女服饰。
The traditional young ladies' dress of Khalkhas.

柯尔克孜族男女头饰。每种头饰都显得富丽堂皇，着
实迷人。
The headgear of Khalkhas people. Every headgear is
magnificent and attractive.

哈萨克族中老年妇女的装束。
The dress of Kazak middle-aged women.

哈萨克族老年人服饰。
The clothing of Kazak elders.

牧区哈萨克族小姑娘的服饰。
The dress of little girls in Kazak pasturing area.

哈萨克族驯鹰者的服饰。The clothing of Kazak eagle trainer.

哈萨克族青年男女服饰。The clothing of Kazak young people.

哈萨克族老年妇女服饰为老人增添了不少姿色。
The Kazak old ladies' dress has added more good looks to the elders.

蒙古族青年妇女服饰。
The dress of Mongolian young ladies.

满族妇女的服饰。The dress of Manchu women.

回族姑娘的服饰和头饰。
The dress and headgear of Hui nationality.

锡伯族男女青年和老人的服饰。 The clothing of young people and elders of Xibo nationality.

达斡尔族老年人的服饰。The elders'clothing of Dawoer nationality.

67

塔吉克族青年男子的服饰。The young men's clothing of Tajik.

塔吉克族妇女的服饰。Tajik nationality women's dress.

俄罗斯族男女服饰。Russian people's clothing.

乌孜别克族妇女服饰。Wuzibieke ladies' dress.

塔塔尔族小姑娘的头饰
Tataer little girls' headgear

69

工艺品
Craftwork

    新疆少数民族的工艺品，犹如一座百花园，琳琅满目，绚丽多彩。人们在衣、食、住、行各个方面无不用艺术的手法和艺术眼光去美化、生产加工各种工艺品。生活是丰富多彩的，而这些精美的工艺品为多彩的生活更加增添了色彩和情趣。

    和田的地毯、艾德莱斯绸和草原牧民花毡等工艺品，是千百年来人们勤劳智慧的结晶。今天，这些灿烂的工艺品仍在美化着人们的生活。而品种繁多的乐器，又为人们生活增添了无穷的欢乐。

    新疆少数民族的工艺品，像一首诗一首歌，把我们带入一个古老纯朴的艺术境界。

    The arts & crafts of Xin Jiang minority are like a kaleidoscope, so colorful and attractive. In every field of living people find the art and create the art. The life is rich and colorful, these arts & crafts have added more color and fun to the life.

    Hetian carpet, Aideliesi silk and herdsmen's flower felt are all the fruit of people's intelligence of thousands of years. Today, these splendid craftworks are still serving our daily life. These various music instruments also give more pleasure to our life.

    The arts & crafts of Xin Jiang minorities are a song, a poem, bringing us into an ancient and pure art world.

和田地毯驰名中外，以其精湛的工艺和独
特的艺术风格被人们所垂青。
Hetian carpet is world-famous, its technique
is exquisite and the art style is distinctive.

维吾尔族妇女用灵巧的双手在编织地毯。
The Uigur women are weaving the carpets
with their skillful hands.

农民用传统的手法纺织艾德莱斯绸。The farmers weaving the Aideliesi silk by the traditional technique.

艾德莱斯绸是维吾尔族妇女最喜欢使用的一种面料。
The Aideliesi silk is the preferred of Uigur women.

英吉沙小刀是以产地英吉沙县而得名。这种佩刀大约有300多年的历史，做工精良，是值得收藏的工艺品。
The Yingjisha knife is famous by the name of Yingjisha county. This wearing knife has the history about more than 300 hundred years. It is elaborately made, and is a craftwork worthy of collection.

维吾尔族师傅加工小刀。
The Uigur masters are making the knives.

哈萨克族折刀。Kazak clasp knives.

维吾尔族妇女绣花帽。
The Uigur women are weaving the flower hats.

花帽市场。Flower hat market.

哈萨克族小姑娘戴的花帽。
The flower hats worn by Kazak girls.

风格不一的回族人的小帽。
The Hui people's hats with different styles.

塔吉克族小姑娘的帽子。
The hats of Tajik girls.

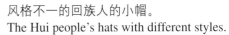

哈萨克族妇女用传统的方法擀毡，擀好后，再用彩色布剪成图案绣上去，这种毡子叫"斯尔玛克"。
Kazak women use traditional way to roll the felts, when finished, cut the color cloth to make the patterns and embroider them on the felts. Thses felts are called "Siermake".

柯尔克孜族的壁挂是工艺十分讲究的一种挂毯，规格大小不等。其绣法有刺绣、贴绣、扎绣、镶附彩绘等，因此显得十分珍贵。
Khalkhas wall hangings are very elaborated on its technique, their sizes are different. Their methods of embroidering including:needlework, gluing, pricking, inlaying. So the hangings are all precious.

维吾尔、哈萨克、柯尔克孜等民族为婴儿专门设计了一种摇床。这种摇床不仅制作精美，同时能使婴儿很快进入梦境。
Uigur, Kazak and Khalkhas have designed a special rocking bed for the infants. It is exquisitely made, and lets the infants sleep soundly.

少数民族妇女天姿美丽，再配上各种项链、耳环、发卡、脖卡、领针、腕卡、手镯、戒指、胸针等各种工艺品来点缀，使其更加美丽动人。
The minority women are born beautifully. The necklace, earring, hairpin, neck pin, collar pin, wrist pin, bracelet, finger ring and brooch, etc., add more beauty to it.

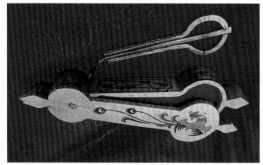

众多的独特乐器，丰富了少数民族的生活。图为维吾尔族的弹拨尔和都塔尔乐器。
The various distinctive music instruments have added more fun to the minorities' living. The picture is the Uigur nationality's music instruments of Tangbaer and Dutaer.

哈萨克族的部分民间乐器。
Part of the folk music instruments of Kazak.

各具特色的各民族乐器。
Various kinds of music instruments of different nationalities.

牧民用精美的工艺来装饰马的鞍具。
The herdsmen decorating their horse saddles with these fancy artworks.

刻有图案的马肚带和马蹬
The horse girths and saddle irons carved with patterns.

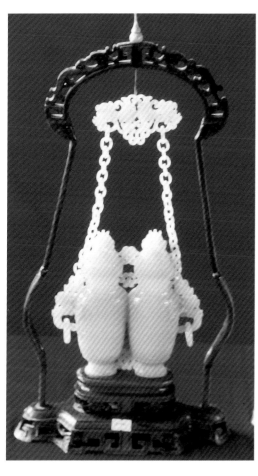

新疆是和田玉的故乡，闻名遐尔的和田玉被誉为玉中的精品。其玉雕造型生动，制作精美，蜚声中外。

Xin Jiang is the native place of Hetian jade, the famous Hetian jade has the honor"the essence of all jades". Its jade carving is lively and fine, well-known to China and abroad.

新疆的陶器中，以喀什的土陶最为驰名。它历史悠久，带有浓郁的乡土气息，表现出特殊的美感和艺术的魅力。

In Xin Jiang's pottery, the Kashi's earthenware is the most famous, which has a long history. It has a strong native breath, and special aesthetic feeling and charm.

体 育
SPORT

　　新疆的民族体育丰富多彩。值得一提的是传统式的体育表演和体育竞赛项目，目前仍保留了古老的体育内容。在牧区人们在马背上创造了许多精彩和富有民族特色的体育文化，这些项目对增进各民族的体质，发挥少数民族的勇敢、机智风格和培养骁勇、无畏的性格，起到了重要作用。体育和生活的环境是不可分隔的，人们结合生活条件，创造了许多体育项目。面积博大的新疆，为开展多彩的民族体育也创造了有利条件，无论哪种体育竞赛和表演都惊心动魄，且饶有风趣，这大概是新疆少数民族体育的特色。

　　The national sports in Xin Jiang are rich and colorful, they still contain the old traditions. In the pasturing areas, people had created many special national sports on horseback, these sports have played an important part to improve the health and train the courage and wittiness of minority people

　　Sport and living are two inseparable parts. Many sports are created in accordance with the living conditions. Xin Jiang has great extent of area, this provides a favorable condition to develop the national sports. Every sport competition and performance are all interesting and thrilling, this is just the feature of Xin Jiang minority sports

"达瓦孜"维吾尔语的意思是"高空走绳",是维吾尔族传统的体育项目之一。

"Dawazi" in Uigur is the meaning "walking on the rope at a high altitude". It is one of the Uigur's traditional sport items,

叼羊是维吾尔、哈萨克、柯尔克孜、塔吉克等民族在马背上进行激烈争夺的一项体育运动。每逢佳节和喜庆的日子里都要举行这种体育活动。

"Diaoyan" is one of the intense sport of Uigur, Kazak, Khalkhas and Tajik on the back of horse. Whenever there is a happy event on the grassland, the herdsmen will carry out this sport.

在柯尔克孜族中，不仅有男人参加叼羊，而且妇女也参加叼羊。
Both men and women of Khalkhas join the sport "Diaoyan".

姑娘追是哈萨克族青年男女在马背上的一项娱乐活动，一般在喜庆的节日举行。如今参加姑娘追的人员，不限于青年男女，已婚的青年人和中年人也都可以参加。

"Girl chasing" is a recreation activity of Kazak young people on horseback, it is generally held on the days of festival. The partners of the activity are not limited to young people, the married or middle-aged people all can join it.

每逢佳节和喜庆的日子里，除赛马外，还举行
赛骆驼、赛毛驴等比赛。
Except horse race, the minority people also hold
camel race, donkey race and so on when in the
festivals.

马背上的角力。也就是在马背上"摔跤",被拉下马背的为败者。
"Wrestling on the horseback", the rider who has been pull down the horseback is defeated.

马背上击棍,是柯尔克孜族传统古老的一项马背上的运动。以把对方击落马下为胜。

"Stick attacking on horseback", it is a traditional horseback activity of Khalkhas. The rider who has beaten the rival off his saddle will win.

骑马拾银元。要求骑马人在飞速奔跑的情况下，弯腰从地上拾起红布包着的银元。

"Picking up the silver coins on horseback", it requires the rider in the speed of the horse stoop down to the ground to pick up the coins wrapped in a red cloth.

骑马钻火圈是近代草原上兴起的一项运动，体现娴熟的马术和骁勇的本领。

"Riding a horse to jump over a fire loop" is a new sport on the grassland, it displays the rider's skilful horsemanship and valiancy.

利用家畜进行竞赛，也是少数民族经常取乐的形式。获胜家畜的主人还能获奖品。
Using the domestic animals to hold the competition is a common way of fun making of minorities. The winner will be prized.

在喜庆的日子，大都举行摔跤比赛。
At any happy events, the wrestling competitions are usually hold.

柯尔克孜族农牧民都喜欢荡秋千，并举行比赛。
Khalkhas farmers and herdsmen all like to play on
the swing, and hold the competition.

空中踏板也是各族青年常来显身手的地方。
"Stepping on the footplates in the air" is also a
sport many young people like to display their
skills..

"萨哈迪尔"是维吾尔族的一项传统体育活动。这项活动类似
转轮秋千。

"Sahadier" is a traditional sport of Uigur. This sport is something
like playing on a swing.

打嘎嘎和打木桩都是青少年喜爱的一种游戏。
"Hitting the Gaga" and "Hitting the wood stake"are all
the favorite games of young people.

南疆农村经常举行的一种棍球比赛。以把球打入对方阵营为胜。
In Nanjiang country a kind of cudgel ball competition is often held,
the team who drives the ball to the gate of rival wins.

少数民族都喜欢用大绳作为一种运动的工具，进行比赛。
Most of the minorities like to use the big ropes as the tool of
sports.

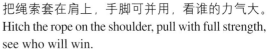

把绳索套在肩上，手脚可并用，看谁的力气大。
Hitch the rope on the shoulder, pull with full strength,
see who will win.

比腕力　Hand wrestling.

锡伯族从小喜爱射箭，因而成为一项群众性的体育运动。
The people of Xibo nationality like archery from childhood, so the archery has become a popular activity.

比臂力　Arm pulling .

俄罗斯族在过复活节时，要举行一种碰鸡蛋的游戏。
When Russians are celebrating the Easter day, they would play an"egg bumping" game.

比脖力　Neck pulling.

丧葬
FUNERAL

　　人死了，离开了人间，总希望有个好的归宿。所以，新疆各少数民族对待丧事是十分隆重的。信仰伊斯兰教的民族丧葬习俗，仍受着宗教的影响，使人们相信，死后可以升天，所以，人们对死亡也并不那么恐惧。

　　新疆少数民族都实行土葬，不陪葬衣物，信奉"光光地来，光光地走"的信条。信仰伊斯兰教的民族，还实行速葬，人去世后，不得超过三天就得安葬。同时还坚持"落叶归根"，在外地去世的人，要运回来安葬在家乡。

　　人去世后，人们还要在3天、7天、40天和周年时进行悼念，每逢节日还要去墓地缅怀悼念，这些都表达了少数民族中人与人之间的深厚的情感。

　　When people die, they hope to have a good place to rest permanently. So Xin Jiang minorities' funerals are all very ceremonious. The funerals of the minorities believing in Islam still being influenced by the religion. They believe that the people will go to heaven after they die, so they are not so fearing about the death.

　　Xin Jiang minorities follow inhumation, nothing is needed to be buried with the dead. They believe the credo"Come alone, go alone"; The Islamic minorities also practise"Fast inhumation", i.e. when a people is dead, not more than three days he has to be buried after the death; And also practise "All falling leaves come back to the ground", if a person dies in the place other than his hometown, his has to be brought back home to be buried in the hometown.

　　On the 3rd day, 7th day, 40th day and anniversary after the death, a mourning ceremony has to be hold, and in every festival people have to go to the grave to recall and mourn for the dead. This expresses the profound feelings existing between the minority people.

11世纪维吾尔族杰出的学者、语言学家马哈穆德·喀什噶尔陵墓，建在疏附县乌帕尔乡。他著有著名的《突厥语大辞典》。

Mahamode Kashigeer, an outstanding scholar and linguist of Uigur in the 11th century, his mausoleum was built in the Wupaer village of Shufu county. One of his famous works is "Turkish dictionary".

玉素甫·哈斯·哈吉甫陵墓建在喀什市区。他是11世纪维吾尔族的诗人、学者和思想家，著有长诗《福乐智慧》。

Yushupu Hasi Hajipu, a Uigur poet, scholar and ideologist in 11th century, his mausoleum was built in the urban of Kashi city. One of his works is the long poem "Blessing wisdom".

阿巴霍加陵墓（香妃墓）位于喀什市，始建于 1640 年前后，是一座十分精美宏伟的伊斯兰古建筑。在阿巴霍加陵墓（香妃墓）背后，有大片普通老百姓的墓。
Abahuojia (the wife of the prince) mausoleum is situated in Kashi city, built in around 1640. It is a beautiful and magnificent Islamic ancient architecture. Behind this mausoleum it is a great extent of common people's graves.

维吾尔族的墓地是集中的，建筑风格也不完全一样。
The Uigur graves are concentrated, with some different architectural styles.

家人去世后，女人要戴白头巾，男人腰里要围白布，对死者表示哀悼。
After one family member passes away, the female should wear white hood,
while the male should tie a white cloth around the waist, to mourn for the dead.

哈萨克族妇女在对死者表达沉痛地哀悼。
The Kazak women are mourning the dead
to express their deep feeling of grief.

死者要安放在灵柩里，并要盖上绣有或印有经文的绿布。
The dead should be put inside the coffin, and covered with the
green cloth on which the scriptures are embroidered or printed.

把死者从家里直接抬往清真寺，请阿訇念经。
The dead is carried from home directly to the mosque, the imam is
invited to chant scriptures.

送到清真寺念经后，才能进行埋葬。
Before burying, the dead should be sent
to the mosque for chanting scriptures.

在入葬之后，阿訇当场介绍死者的生平，并要向送葬的人询问死者是否有债务，若有债务，由亲属来归还。
After burying, the imam and the dead's dependents or relatives have to introduce the stories of dead's life, and ask the people attending the funeral if the dead has any debt remained. If yes, the debt should be paid back by the dead's dependents.

参加送葬的都是男子，妇女不去送。等宗教仪式结束后，才能开始安葬。
The people attending the funeral are all men, instead of women. It can not start the burying until the religious ceremony is finished.

死者去世3天、7天、40天和周年时要举行"乃孜尔"(祭事)，对死者进行悼念。每逢古尔邦节、肉孜节，亲属还要到坟地去缅怀死者。

On the 3rd day, 7th day, 40th day and anniversary after the death, the "Naizier"(memorial ceremony) should be hold to mourn for the dead. When Guerban day and Fast-breaking day are coming, the dead's dependents and relatives should go to mosque and grave to recall the dead.

穆斯林去世举行"乃孜尔"，这天要做抓饭进行施舍。这是哈萨克族牧民在过"乃孜尔"。

When a Muslem is dead, the "Naizier" ccremony has to be hold, and cook the "grasping food" on the same day for alms. This is the Kazak herdsmen celebrating the "Naizier".

不管天气多么寒冷，到了哀悼死者的日期，哈萨克人都要按时进行悼念，表达了哈萨克人对死者执著的感情。
No matter how cold the weather is, when the mourning day comes, Kazaks have to mourn on time, to express the inflexible feelings to the dead.

哈萨克族用石头垒成的墓，外形像一匹骏马。
Kazak graves built by the laying of stones look like a steed.

哈萨克族的墓是根据居住的自然条件来建造的，大都呈圆形，像一座毡房。
The Kazak graves are all built according to the natural conditions at the living place, most of the graves are round, look like a felt house.

哈萨克族用木材建造的墓，仍像毡房。死者埋在土中，木架是外面的保护层。
A Kazak grave built with wood still looks like a felt house. The dead is buried into the ground, the wood rack is the exterior protection of the grave.

回族乡亲在清真寺为死者默哀，愿真主保佑、安息。
The Hui villagers are mourning in the mosque, wishing the Allah's blessing, and rest in peace.

穆斯林去世后，都要将尸体洗净，并缠上白纱布才能去清真寺和安葬。
After the death of a Muslem, the body of the dead has to be cleaned, and wrapped with white gauze, then bring it to the mosque and buried.

回族人去世后，都送往回民的清真寺请阿訇念经。
After the death of a Hui people, the dead should be sent to the mosquer and let the imam to chant scriptures for the dead.

信仰伊斯兰教的群众都实行土葬，墓坑深挖到2米时，侧面还要挖一个洞，把死者安放在那里。

The people believing in Islam will carry out inhumation. When the pit is as deep as two meters, one hole on the side of the pit has to be dig, then the dead is put into hole.

柯尔克孜人埋葬前，其亲属向死者遗体告别。

Before the dead of Khalkhas is buried, the independents and relatives pay the last respects to the dead.

塔吉克族在埋葬死者时，不允许妇女靠近，从挖坑到埋葬全部由男人完成。同时在挖坑时，上面还要有人绷上布，不愿叫外人看到埋葬时的情景。

When the dead is buried by Tajiks, no woman is allowed to come close. The men finish the work from digging the pit to burying the dead. When in digging, the site has to be covered by cloth, disliking to be seen when burying.

塔吉克人在阿訇给死者念完经之后，把死者放在一个木架上，并迅速抬到墓地安葬。

When Imam has finished chanting scriptures for the dead, the Tajiks put the dead on a wood rack, and some people lift the dead to the grave for burying.

塔吉克人去世后,其死者家属和亲戚在头上要缠上绿色的布,并哭泣表示哀悼。塔吉克人家里有了丧事,亲朋好友都要来探望安慰,男人见面时,有的还要敬烟。

When a Tajik has died, his dependents and relatives have to tie a green cloth on the heads, and crying for the mourning.When a Tajik family has the funeral arrangements, their friends and relatives will come to visit and comfort, and men will propose the cigarettes to each other when meet.

塔吉克族妇女在死者去世周年时,要去墓地悼念死者。参加悼念的妇女都要围上白头巾,表示对死者的尊重。

The Tajik women have to go to the grave to mourn for the dead when comes the anniversary of the death. The women attending the morning ceremony should wear the white hoods, to express their respect to the dead.

俄罗斯人在给死者上坟时,还要带上点心和甜米饭,大家互相赠送并默哀。

When Russians are visiting the grave, they would bring some refreshment and sweet rice, presenting to each other and stand in silent tribute.

俄罗斯族有自己的墓地,不允许其他民族葬在其内。俄罗斯人实行土葬,在墓后面还要立碑,记录死者的姓名和去世的年月。

Russians have their own graves, the other nations would not be allowed to bury inside. Russia carries out the inhumation, and a gravestone is stood behind the grave, to record the name of the dead and his date of death.

人生礼仪
ETIQUETTE

　　新疆少数民族的礼仪，充分表达了新疆各民族之间的友好关系和热情好客的性格。

　　维吾尔族群众说："我们的桌子始终是铺得很宽的"，哈萨克牧民说："祖先遗留下来的财产中，一半是客人的"。这些热情好客的语言，保证了每位到新疆来的客人将受到热情接待和尊重。

　　新疆是多民族地区，各种宗教信仰得到充分尊重，各民族之间和在本民族之间的友好相助蔚然成风。在饮酒、吃肉、待客等方面的礼仪也表达了各民族的热情和好客的风格。

　　在新疆不用发愁，不会寂寞，那热情的民族礼仪，足叫您快乐、无忧。

The Xin Jiang minorities' etiquettes fully represent the kindness and friendship between different people or different nationalities.

The Uigur people say: "Our table are always the broadest", while the Kazak Herdsmen say: "The half of the properties left behind from the ancestors belong to our guests". These expressions can make sure that the people who are visiting in Xin Jiang will be warmly received

Xin Jiang is a multinational area, different religions have all been respected and reserved, there is a good friendship between different nationalities. Also the etiquettes of drinking wine, eating meat, treating guests and so on have expressed the warm and friendship of different nationalities

You wouldn't need to worry and wouldn't be alone when you are in Xin Jiang, the warm ettiquttes of all nationalities will make you happy and worry-free

长期居住在新疆的维吾尔、哈萨克、回族等民族信仰伊斯兰教，宗教信仰是他们生活的重要部分。每逢古尔邦、肉孜节时，穆斯林群众都要去清真寺作礼拜，以求新的一年平安、幸福。

The nationalities of Uigur, Kazak, Hui and so on living in Xin Jiang all believe in Islem. Religion is a main part of their living. When on Corban day or Fast-breaking day, all Muslem people have to go to Mosque to worship, to imprecate for the peace and happy in the new year.

每日五次祈祷，是穆斯林的一项重要"功修"，出门在外，到了时间也得祈祷。
To pray five times per day, is an important moral cultivation of Muslem. Even going out, he should pray when it is the time for praying.

自费乘飞机出国朝觐。　The Muslem people going abroad by airplane to worship at their own expenses.

维吾尔族男人之间见面时行施的捂胸礼。
The Uigur men's etiquette of covering the chest by hand when meeting each other.

维吾尔族妇女相互见面时若是亲近的要拥抱，并要左右贴一下脸面。
When meeting each other, the Uigur women would hug each other if they have a close relation, and touch their faces both on the left and right one time each.

柯尔克孜族妇女见面时，也施贴面礼。
When Khalkhas women meet, they also follow the face-touching etiquette.

哈萨克族妇女见了晚辈施亲吻礼。
The Kazak women will kiss their juniors when meet.

塔吉克族男女见面礼　The etiquette when Tajik man and woman meet.

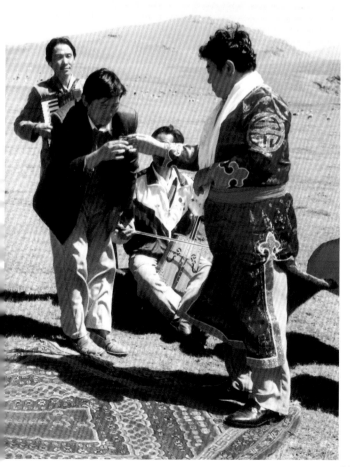

蒙古人是注重礼仪的民族，来了客人要献哈达，表示尊重。另外还要给客人敬酒，表达欢迎和祝福的意思。

Mongolia is a nationality pays good attention to etiquette. When guests come, they will present a hada to express their respect, and also propose a toast to the guests, to express welcome and good wishes.

111

哈萨克人遇到喜庆的日子，要搞一种叫〝恰秀〞的仪式。
When in the days of happy events, the Kazaks will hold a ceremony called "Qiaxiu".

有朋友自远方来，是高兴的事情。哈萨克族女阿肯弹起了冬布拉，俄罗斯族姑娘跳起了踢踏舞，维吾尔族小孩为外国朋友跳起了舞蹈。
The friends have come afar, it is a happy thing for the minorities. The Kazak women playing Dongbula, the Russian girls dancing tap dance, the Uigur children presenting a dance for the friends from abroad.

草原上的民族，在待客时，要举行一种"巴塔"的仪式，即把要宰的羊带到客厅，主人要向客人祝福，客人也要向主人祝福，之后才能把羊拉出去宰杀。

The nationalities on the grassland will hold a "Bata" ceremony when in treating the guests. They bring the sheep going to be slaughtered to the drawing room, the host blesses good wishes to the guest, and the guest to the host too, then the sheep is brought out to be slaughtered.

"割礼"是信仰伊斯兰教群众的一种"托衣"（喜事），男孩到了7岁左右，要进行"割礼"（割去包皮）。这天，家里要请客，大家来祝贺。这是回族男孩在"割礼"之前。

"Circumcision" is a "Tuoyi"(happy event) of the Islamic people in Xin Jiang. The boys in the age around 7 have to be circumcised. In this day, the guests would be invited to the home to celebrate the event. This is the Hui boys before the "Circumcision" ceremony.

蒙古族有祭敖包的习俗，敖包作为地界、标志在新疆已保存多年。人们相互在敖包见面，在敖包洒酒、饮酒，表示对亡灵的缅怀。

Mongolians have the tradition of holding a memorial ceremony to the Aobao. As a boundary and landmark, Aobao has many yeas of history in Xin Jiang. People meet each other at Aobao, spaying and drinking wine there, to recall the deads.

维吾尔、哈萨克、柯尔克孜等民族都有驯鹰、养鹰的传统。
Uigur, Kazak and Khalkhas all have the tradition of breeding and training eagles.

哈萨克族牧民对路过或搬迁来的牧民都要伸出援助之手。
Kazak herdsmen would give a helping hand to the other herdsmen passing by or moving to nearby from other place.

维吾尔族喜欢花，并有男女戴花、持花的习俗。
Uigurs like flowers very much, both men and women wear or bring flowers.

门上挂个布条，表示女人生孩子或其他事，请外人免入。
If a piece of cloth is hanged on a door, it means that the woman is having a baby or other things, no admitting.

谁家有了婚丧之事，大家都要去看望或帮助。
Whenever there is a happy event or funeral arrangements in a family, everybody will go to visit and help.

过去锡伯族记事全靠记事结，发生重大事情，用布条或绳子结在记事结上。
In the past, the Xibo nationality records the important events by tie a piece of cloth or a rope on a cord.

节 日
FESTIVAL

节日是信仰的寄托，也是为了纪念。新疆信仰伊斯兰教民族的节日，是由宗教习俗而转变为节日的。在古尔邦、肉孜、努鲁孜等节日中，人们期盼来年的幸福和安宁，举行盛大的庆祝活动，宰杀牲畜、制作糕点，穿着民族服装，走亲访友、载歌载舞，成了节日的主要内容。

举行赛马、叼羊、姑娘追、摔跤、射箭则是牧区和农村过节中不可缺少的项目，从通过体育表演和游戏来表达他们的欢乐心情。

人们在欢乐的时刻，也不会忘记为今天生活而养育了自己的先辈，他们要去扫墓悼念，缅怀前辈和友好的功绩及恩德。

Festival is the variant of religion, it has the same purpose of celebration. The festivals of the nationalities believing in Islam are come from the religious ceremony. In the festivals of Corban day, Fast-breaking day, Nuluzi day and so on, people are expecting the happy and peace in coming years. They hold grand celebrations, slaughtering livestock, making cakes, wearing national clothes, visiting relatives and friends, dancing and singing, these are the main contents of the festivals.

The horse racing, Diaoyan, girl chasing, wrestling and archery are the indispensable sport items when in the festivals of pasturing areas and villages. People can express their happy emotions through these sports or recreations.

In this happy moment, people would not forget their ancestors who had fostered them with great hardships. They have to go to pay respect to their ancestors' graves, recall their good deeds and credits.

载歌载舞欢庆节日
Singing and dancing to celebrate the festival.

古尔邦节、肉孜节是信仰伊斯兰教民族的重要节日，吐鲁番的维吾尔族群众在苏公塔上吹起长号为节日增添气氛。
The Gorban day and Fast-breaking day are the important festivals of Islamic nationalities. Uigur people in Tulufang blowing trombone on Sugong tower to celebrate the festival.

维吾尔族群众在节日里身着民族盛装翩翩起舞，表达自己欢乐的心情。
In the festival, the Uigur people putting on national costume singing and dancing, to express their happy emotion.

努鲁孜节，也是信仰伊斯兰教民族的主要节日。节日这天要做有7种食品混合而成的"努鲁孜"饭，以示年年富足有余。
Nuluzi day, a main festival of Islamic nationalities. In this day, the "Nuluzi food" which contains 7 kinds of foodstuff is being made, to express the happy years they have had.

节日里，哈萨克族妇女准备好丰富的食品并烧好醇香的奶茶，招待客人。

In the festival, The Kazak women will prepare the abundant food and mellow wine to treat the guests.

节日期间，草原上常常还要举行马上表演。 In the festival, there will be an on-horseback performance held on the grassland.

节日里，哈萨克族要搞一种叫"恰秀"的仪式，由年长中德高望重的妇女把食品撒向人群，意为把幸福和快乐撒向人间。
Kazak people will hold a "Qiaxiu" ceremony in the festival, some senior women throw the foodstuff to the crowd, it means that to throw the happy to the world.

哈萨克族老年妇女，在节日里都穿着传统的"开米赛克"。
The old women of Kazak will put on traditional "Kaimisaike" in the festival.

节日里或是祭日，穆斯林群众还在树枝或是专门搭起的树枝上，系上白、红等颜色的布条，以示悼念亡灵。
In the day of festival or memorial ceremony, the Muslim people tie the white or red pieces of cloth on the tree branches, to mourn for the deads.

节日里，达斡尔人在树枝上系上布条，悼念先祖。
In the festival, Dawoer people tie the pieces of cloth on the tree branches to mourn for their ancestors.

维吾尔、塔吉克族每年农历8月15日晚上都举行一种传统的祭典。祭典之夜，他们用棉花捻子和草扎成的灯，全家围坐在一起，祈求真主保佑平安，农牧业丰收。
Uigur and Tajik will hold a traditional ceremony on 15th of Aug. of lunar calendar. In the night of the festival, they make the lanterns with cotton twists and grass, all family members sit together to pray the blessing from Allah to have a good harvest.

124

抹黑节是锡伯族传统有趣的节日。每逢农历正月16日的清晨，人们往脸上抹黑，是为了祈求五谷之神不要把黑穗病传到人间，以求农业丰收。

"Black smearing day" is an interesting festival of Xibo nationality. In the morning of 16th day of first month in every lunar year, people put the black on their faces, for the purpose to pray the God of Crops don't bring the dustbrand to the earth, and beg for a good harvest.

每年的农历10月13日，是满族的传统节日——颁金节。"颁金"是满语，意为满族命名之日。

October 13 of each lunar year is the Banjin day, a traditional festival of Manchu nationality. "Banjin"is Manchu language means "Manchu naming"

帕斯喀节，也称"复活节"，是俄罗斯族的传统节日。人们尽情娱乐，使节日呈现在一片欢乐之中。

Pasika day, or called Easter, is a traditional festival of Russia. People enjoy themselves in this festival.

撒班节是塔塔尔民族的传统节日。每年6月中旬，人们选择风景区举行各种体育比赛及文艺活动。

Saban day is a traditional festival of Tataer nationality. In the June of each year, people select a beauty spot to hold different sports and recreations.

图书在版编目（CIP）数据

中国新疆民俗大观／新疆美术摄影出版社编．－乌鲁木齐：新疆美术摄影出版社，2001.6
ISBN 7-80658-063-8

Ⅰ.中⋯　Ⅱ.新⋯　Ⅲ.少数民族风俗习惯－新疆
－摄影集　Ⅳ.K892.445-64

中国版本图书馆 CIP 数据核字(2001) 第 031435 号

中国新疆民俗大观（中、英文对照）

出版发行: 新 疆 美 术 摄 影 出 版 社
（乌鲁木齐市西宏路 118 号　邮编: 830000）
制　作: 深圳市万里红印刷设计有限公司
印　刷: 深 圳 宝 峰 印 刷 有 限 公 司
开　本: 1/16　889 × 1230(mm)
印　张: 8　　字数: 15 千字
版　次: 2001 年 6 月第 1 版　2001 年 6 月第 1 次印刷
印　数: 1-3500 册
ISBN 7-80658-063-8/J·035　　定价: ￥98.00 元